THE COUNTRY CUPBOARD

Herbs

THE COUNTRY CUPBOARD

HERBS

IMAGINATIVE TIPS & SENSIBLE ADVICE FOR COOKING, GROWING, AND ENJOYING

PAT ROSS

Watercolors by Carolyn Bucha

FRIEDMAN/FAIRFAX
PUBLISHERS

A FRIEDMAN/FAIRFAX BOOK

Library of Congress Cataloging-in-Publication data

Ross, Pat, 1943–
    The country cupboard: herbs / by Pat Ross; watercolors by
Carolyn Bucha.
        p.   cm.
    ISBN 1-56799-871-2
    1. Cookery (Herbs)   2. Herbs.   I. Title.
TX819.H4R665   1999
641.6'57—dc21   99-19990
    CIP

Editor: Reka Simonsen
Art Director: Jeff Batzli
Designer: Andrea Karman
Production Manager: Karen Matsu Greenberg

Color separations by Colourscan Overseas Co Pte Ltd
Printed in Hong Kong by Midas Printing Limited

1 3 5 7 9 10 8 6 4 2

For bulk purchases and special sales, please contact:
Friedman/Fairfax Publishers
Attention: Sales Department
15 West 26th Street
New York, New York 10010
212/685-6610   FAX 212/685-1307

Visit our website:
http://www.metrobooks.com

This book is intended as a reference volume only, not as a medical manual or guide to self-treatment. Do not attempt self-diagnosis or medication without seeking the assistance of a competent physician.

Acknowledgments

I'm particularly indebted to my talented friend, Gail Rock, whose savvy on the subject of herbs has provided depth and balance to this book.

As usual, my publisher, Michael Friedman, has outdone himself in producing a beautiful volume—and in putting it out to all the right places. Sharyn Rosart continues to add her untiring support while Reka Simonsen has become a welcome and vital part of the team on this Country Cupboard series. Also, many thanks to Helen Johnson for her enthusiastic publicity efforts, and to David Drachman for understanding what Carolyn and I are up to.

This pretty picture is complete because of the prodigious talent of Carolyn Bucha, whose artwork continues to graces the pages of the Country Cupboard series. Both Carolyn and I would like to thank the designer, Andrea Karman, and the most creative art director, Jeff Batzli, for putting it all together.

Contents

Introduction

Every civilization in history has used herbs to season and preserve food. Although many souvenirs of herb history no longer relate directly to our modern lives, the little-known facts are fascinating. The ancient Egyptians used mint as a digestive aid. Thus, when I pop an after-dinner mint into my mouth, I can reflect on my participation in a tradition that's five thousand years old. Today, most cooks use herbs to season foods on a daily basis to enhance the taste and explore the culinary possibilities. In times past, herbs were essential for preserving meats and masking the taste of less-than-fresh foods. Now we season our party snacks with chili for flair only, and we can feel fortunate indeed that the rest is history.

Until the nineteenth century, herbs were humankind's primary source of medicine. In a fair share of Western movies, it is the amazing poultice of herbs and roots that saves a limb or cures the hero of a near-fatal concussion. Garlic worn around one's neck was thought to ward off both disease and evil spirits. Today, garlic—in several forms—is making a comeback for the treatment of colds and the flu. For centuries, monasteries were a wellspring of herbal knowledge, as monks carefully recorded not only their lists of herbal remedies, but also the designs of their "physic" gardens. When you consider how important herbs have been historically, it becomes difficult to look at the array of fresh herbs in the market without appreciating the scope of such a seemingly simple subject.

Every good cook knows his or her way around the herbal neighborhood. In fact, every great cuisine I can think of has made extensive use of herbs for seasoning; herbs are simply indispensable in recreating authentic ethnic recipes. Italian spaghetti sauce would be flat and uninteresting without the generous amount of fresh sweet basil that we all love. And how could I make my zesty avocado salad without the earthy flavor of cilantro and the bite of fresh red chilies? If I'm pressed for time, I can toss herbs into my simplest dishes and everyone thinks I've been in the kitchen for hours. I love to swap recipes with friends, so I've included some favorites in this book, a happy mix of everything from herbed mayonnaise to roast chicken with thyme and mustard. Every year, I make herb vinegars in pretty bottles to give as gifts. Each bottle looks so beautiful that I have trouble parting with it.

I'm starting an herb garden from scratch at my newly rebuilt farmhouse in Virginia. It's exciting to have such a tabula rasa provided by the acres of available land; it's also quite a challenge to get it right. I settled on having a modest herb garden to begin with, planting just a few of my favorite herbs in a sunny spot close to the kitchen door. Because I like the notion of discovering herbs in more distant parts of the garden as well, I've scattered a few among the perennials that grow along the fine stone wall beyond my terrace, which is a pleasant stroll from the house. There, the parsley and thyme will create a pretty and fragrant carpet. During the growing season, I'm on the lookout for good gardening advice, much of which I've happily passed along in this book. I harvest, preserve, and store a small quantity of herbs—nothing like the stockpiling that our ancestors had to do—but whatever I manage to save gives me the greatest satisfaction. When winter approaches, I know I'll miss the fresh herbs in my garden, so I bring as many potted herbs indoors as the sunny windowsills allow.

With my herbs so close at hand, I need little more than a pair of scissors and a twist of ribbon to come up with a quick and pretty gift. Books about creating gifts of any kind can be enormously frustrating if the gifts are complicated or overly time-consuming, so I've kept any such tips short and sweet. Luckily, herbs are so wonderfully aromatic that they hardly need an elaborate presentation. Some of the gifts in this book are designed for personal care, such as the herbal bath formulas, facial refreshers, and other delicious forms of pampering. My advice is to remember that charity begins at home.

Home decors rich with herbal themes make for warm, inviting places, so start thinking of herbs as another special type of decorative detail, as I have. Using herbs in this way is as simple as hanging a bay wreath in the kitchen or tucking a fresh, aromatic sprig into a linen napkin. Your guests will smile and think, "There's rosemary; that's for remembrance," and they'll recall this special touch for years to come.

—*Pat Ross*

chapter one

Herbs in the Kitchen

ADVICE FOR THE COOK

We've come a long way since the little snip of parsley of our parents' and grand-parents' days, that refreshing minced herb saved for special salads and Sunday potatoes. Today, we benefit from the wisdom of the ancient peoples of Africa, Asia, and the Americas on a more regular basis. Our ancestors considered herbs to be so precious that they used them as currency; in fact, wars were sometimes started over who had the herbs and who did not. I trust this book won't provoke any disturbances, global or otherwise, as we pop fresh and dried herbs into our daily dishes. Here are some tips to keep in mind.

✦ Fresh herbs are always preferable, but dried herbs may be substituted in most recipes. Remember that dried herbs have a much stronger flavor, so you will need less. A rule of thumb is that ½ teaspoon (2.5ml) of dried or ¼ teaspoon (1ml) of powdered herbs is equal to 2 teaspoons (10ml) of minced fresh herbs.

✦ Fresh herbs should be minced, crushed, or cut just before using to release their fullest flavor.

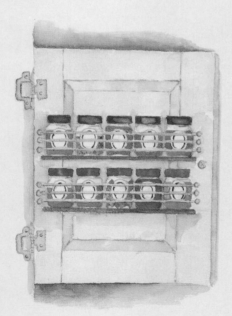

The business of the day is done,
   The last-left hay-maker is gone.
And from the thyme upon the height,
   And from the elder-blossom white,
And pale dog-roses in the hedge,
   And from the mint plant in the sedge,
In puffs of balm the night-air blows
   The perfume which the day fore-goes

                 Matthew Arnold

✦ Buy dried and powdered herbs in the smallest possible quantities, since they go stale relatively quickly. They should be stored in airtight jars in a cool, dark place—not near the heat of the stove, nor on a rack out in the light of the kitchen. A spice rack may be a cute decorating accent, but it does no good for the herbs. You might try storing them on a door rack on the inside of a cupboard away from the stove, or on a revolving rack on a corner shelf.

And thou beholdest the Earth blackened;
then, when We send down water upon it,
it quivers, and swells, and puts forth herbs of every joyous kind.

The Koran

✦ When a jar of herbs has lost its color and aroma, the time has come to replace it.

✦ Recipes often call for *fines herbes*, the classic French mixture of chopped parsley, chervil, and tarragon, with the optional addition of chives. However, many cooks improvise on this combination, using mixtures of their own.

✦ A *bouquet garni* is a bundle of seasoning herbs enclosed in a muslin or cheesecloth bag and used to flavor dishes during cooking. The bag is removed and discarded when the dish is served. The traditional French bouquet consists of thyme, parsley, and bay leaf, but you can experiment with your favorite herbs to create unique bouquets of your own. You can purchase the little muslin bags at most herbalist shops and homeopathic pharmacies, or you can simply cut a square of clean cheesecloth and tie up the corners to make one yourself.

✦ Don't be afraid to experiment with herbs—just make sure to correct the seasoning as you cook. Taste the sauce or dish as you go, making sure you have not used too much or too little of anything, even if you're following the recipe exactly. Batches of herbs differ in intensity, and vegetables and meats can differ in flavor at different times as well.

✦ Until you have some experience in cooking with herbs, add them sparingly. You can always add more, but it's difficult to tone down an over-seasoned dish.

HERB SEASONING GUIDE: AN ALPHABETICAL LISTING

Following is a list of herbs and the foods that go well with them. This list is meant to provide suggestions, but of course some of the best combinations are left to serendipity.

Anise (seeds or leaves):

Beef, cabbage, carrots, chicken, cakes, cookies, eggs, fish, fruit, pastries, pork, salad dressings and garnishes, spinach

Basil:

Beef, broccoli, cabbage, carrots, cauliflower, eggplant, eggs, fish, game, green beans, lamb, pasta, pesto, pizza, potatoes, poultry, rice, salads and salad dressings, shellfish, squash, spinach, tomatoes, veal

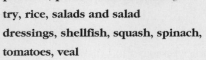

Bay leaf (remove from the dish before serving):

Beans, beef, chicken, fish, lamb, pâté, sauces, soups, stews, stocks, stuffings, tomatoes, veal

Borage:

Chicken, cold soups, fish, iced tea, pickles, salads

Caraway (seeds):

Beef, breads, cabbage or sauerkraut, cauliflower, cheese, coleslaw, eggs, fish, green beans, meatloaf, noodles, peas, pork, potato salad, potatoes, spinach, squash

Cardamom:

Baked apples, cakes, cookies, curries, fruit dishes, gingerbread, ice cream, jams and jellies, meatballs, pastries, pumpkin pie, rice pilaf, squash, sweet potatoes, tea

Chervil:

Beef, carrots, chicken, corn, eggs, fish, peas, potatoes, salads, sauces, spinach, tomatoes, veal

Chervil eaten in salad when they are green,

    with oil and vinegar,

by the agreeableness of their taste,

    are better than other salads through the sweetnesss of their aroma,

and nothing is healthier for weak stomachs.

John Gerard

Chives:
Asparagus, carrots, cauliflower, corn, dips, eggs, fish, peas, potatoes, poultry, salads, soups, spinach, veal

Cilantro (fresh coriander leaves):
Avocados, bean salad, curries, eggs, fish, game, lamb, mushrooms, pâté, pork, potatoes, poultry, salads, salsas, sauces, soups, stews, stir-fries, tomatoes

Coriander (seeds):
Curries, cookies, eggplant, pickles, roast pork, salad dressings, shellfish, soups, spice cakes

Cumin:
Avocados, beans, beef, cabbage, carrots, cauliflower, chicken, curries, dips, lamb, pork, salsas

Dill (fresh):
Avocados, carrots, cucumbers, dips, eggs, fish and fish salads, green beans, lamb, potatoes, pickles, pork, poultry, salad and salad dressings, sauces, soups, squash, stews

Dill (seeds):
Breads, crackers, pickles, salad dressings, sauces, soups, stews

Many of the virtures fennel seed displays,
First, fever in its presence never stays;
Next, it kills poison and the stomach frees,
And last, to human sight gives increased ease.

Regimen Sanitatis Salerni, 10th-century Italy

Fennel (fresh or seeds):
Breads, fish, fruit desserts, meatloaf,
pasta, salads, sauces, sausages, soups,
stews, stuffings

Garlic:
This favorite aromatic ingredient is the
star seasoning of the kitchen—use to
flavor everything from hors d'oeuvres
to ice cream.

Ginger:
Asparagus, beef, carrots, eggplant,
fish, fruit, lamb, marinades, pork,
poultry, soups, squash, stir-fries,
tea, veal

Lemongrass:
Chicken, curries, fish, marinades, pork,
sauces, soups, stews, tea

Lemon verbena:
Chicken, cocktails,
fish, fruit, jams,
marinades,
puddings,
salad dressings,
shellfish, tea

Lovage:
Meats, pâté, potatoes,
poultry, soups, stews,
stuffings, tomatoes

Parsley:

Another all-star that goes with just about everything.

Rosemary:

Beef, breads, eggs, fish, green beans, lamb, marinades, mushrooms, peas, pork, potatoes, poultry, soups, squash, stews, stuffings, veal

Marjoram:

Beef, cabbage, carrots, cauliflower, eggplant, eggs, fish, green beans, lamb, lentils and beans, mushrooms, pasta, poultry, sausages, squash, stuffings, tomatoes, veal

Saffron:

Chicken, corn, eggs, fish, lamb, pork, rice, shell-fish, soups, stews

Mint:

Carrots, desserts, eggplant, fruit drinks, fruit salads and soups, green beans, lamb, lentils and beans, peas, sauces, tabbouleh, tea, veal

Sage:

Asparagus, beans, beef, cabbage, carrots, corn, eggplant, eggs, fish, game, green beans, ham, pâté, peas, pork, potatoes, poultry, sauces, sausage, soups, squash, stews, stuffings, tomatoes, veal

Oregano:

Beans, beef, broccoli, chicken, eggplant, eggs, fish, green beans, lamb, mushrooms, pasta, pork, potatoes, salad dressings, sauces, soups, squash, stews, tomatoes and tomato sauces

Pale saffron plot
    Forget him not;
His dwelling made trim
    look shortly for him.
When harvest is gone
    then saffron comes on;
A little of ground
    brings saffron a pound.

Thomas Tusser

Thyme:

Asparagus, beef, broccoli, carrots,
corn, dried beans, eggplant, eggs,
fish, game, green beans, lamb,
mushrooms, peas, poultry, rice,
spinach, stuffings, tomatoes, veal,
vegetable soup

Turmeric:

Curries, eggs, pickles, rice, salad
dressings, yellow vegetables

Summer savory:

Asparagus, beef, brussels sprouts,
cabbage, carrots, cauliflower, dried
beans, eggplant, eggs, fish, game,
green beans, peas, poultry, salad
dressings, sausage, squash,
tomatoes, veal

Tarragon:

Asparagus, beef, broccoli, carrots,
cauliflower, chicken, eggs, fish, lamb,
mushrooms, peas, potatoes, poultry, rice,
salad dressings, sauces, tomatoes

Are you going to Scarborough Fair?

Parsley, sage, rosemary, and thyme,

Remember me to one who lives there,

She once was a true love of mine.

English folk song

RECIPES STARRING HERBS

I want to share some favorite recipes—
from dips to main courses—where the
herbs are the stars. Some of these recipes
are personal favorites, and others are
beloved dishes passed along by friends
and relatives.

Herb Vinegars

Delicious herb vinegars are easy to
make. Wash and dry fresh herbs, and
place them in a sterilized jar. Cover with
high-quality vinegar of at least 5%
acidity. Cider, red wine, white wine,
rice wine, and sherry vinegars are all
good choices, but avoid using distilled
white vinegar, since it has no flavor.
Use a non-metallic lid (a plastic top or a
cork will do), and store the jar in a cool,
dark location for two weeks, shaking
the jar every few days. Check for flavor
and aroma, and leave it another week
or two if it has not yet attained the
desired strength.

Strain the liquid, and discard the
old herbs. Bring the vinegar to a boil.
Place 2 or 3 fresh sprigs of the same
herbs in another sterilized bottle, pour
in the warm vinegar, and seal. You may
want to add a touch of food coloring
to enhance the appearance. Try these
combinations:

Tarragon in red wine vinegar

**Basil, oregano, and thyme in red wine
vinegar**

Rosemary in white wine vinegar

Chive flowers in white wine vinegar

**Lemongrass and garlic in rice wine
vinegar**

Thyme and garlic in sherry vinegar

Salads, Dressings, and Sauces

DILLED CUCUMBERS IN SOUR CREAM

2 large cucumbers, peeled and thinly sliced

3 radishes, thinly sliced

1½ teaspoons (7.5ml) salt

1 cup (250ml) sour cream

2 tablespoons (30ml) lemon juice

1 tablespoon (15ml) minced onion

2 tablespoons (30ml) chopped dill pickle

1 tablespoon (15ml) drained capers

1½ teaspoons (7.5ml) minced fresh dill

¼ teaspoon (1.25ml) sugar

Dash of pepper

Lightly toss cucumbers with 1 teaspoon (5ml) salt; refrigerate until well chilled. Combine sour cream, lemon juice, remaining salt, onion, radishes, dill pickle, sugar, and pepper. Reserve half of this mixture for garnish. Drain liquid from chilled cucumbers, toss with remaining sour cream mixture, and refrigerate. Serve with reserved sour cream mixture spooned over cucumbers, and garnish with chopped fresh dill. Makes approximately 5 cups (1.25l).

AVOCADO SALAD

½ avocado, cubed

¼ red onion, sliced

2 shallots, sliced

10 parsley leaves

10 cilantro leaves

2 small fresh red chilies, seeded and chopped

5 pitted green olives, quartered

1 large tomato, peeled and diced

3 tablespoons (45ml) sherry vinegar dressing (see below)

Combine all ingredients, and toss with dressing. Serves 2.

Sherry Vinegar Dressing

¼ cup (60ml) extra virgin olive oil

1 tablespoon (15ml) rice wine vinegar

1 tablespoon (15ml) dry sherry

1 teaspoon (5ml) sugar

Salt and pepper to taste

Combine ingredients in small jar, cover, and shake to blend. Makes approximately ⅓ cup (75ml).

FRESH HERB MAYONNAISE

½ cup (125ml) mayonnaise

1 teaspoon (5ml) minced fresh chives

1 teaspoon (5ml) minced fresh dill

1 teaspoon (5ml) minced fresh scallion (white part only)

1 teaspoon (5ml) minced fresh tarragon

Whisk the herbs into the mayonnaise, and garnish with fresh sprigs of dill and tarragon. Excellent on turkey, cold roast chicken, tuna, or hard-cooked eggs or for spicing up your favorite sandwich. Makes approximately ½ cup (125ml).

PESTO

4 cups (250ml) fresh basil leaves, tightly packed

2 teaspoons (10ml) salt

1 teaspoon (5ml) freshly ground black pepper

4 teaspoons (20ml) minced garlic

2 cups (500ml) pine nuts (or English walnuts)

2–2½ cups (500–750ml) extra virgin olive oil

2 cups (500ml) grated fresh Parmesan cheese

In an electric blender, combine small batches of basil, nuts, olive oil, salt, pepper, and garlic. Puree, stopping at 10-second intervals to push ingredients down into blades with a rubber spatula. The mixture should be slightly runny; if it's too thick, dribble in more olive oil. Blend in small batches, pouring each finished batch into a bowl. If serving fresh, stir in the Parmesan cheese. If freezing the pesto, do not add Parmesan until pesto is thawed and ready to serve. Serve on pasta, pizza, or steamed vegetables, or spread it on your favorite sandwiches. Makes about 3 cups (750ml).

Young fairies perched in Rosemary Branches,
while their elders danced in the Thyme.

Vernon Quinn

Soups

HERBED CARROT SOUP

1 onion, chopped

2 cloves of garlic, minced

2 tablespoons (30ml) butter or margarine

1 tablespoon (15ml) minced fresh thyme

6 medium carrots, diced

2 medium potatoes, diced

2 stalks celery, diced

5 sprigs cilantro

6 cups chicken broth

1 bay leaf

Freshly ground black pepper to taste

Cook the onion and garlic in the butter until soft and lightly browned, about 5 minutes. Add the thyme, carrots, potatoes, celery, cilantro, broth, bay leaf, and pepper. Bring to a boil, lower heat,

cover, and simmer until the vegetables are tender. Cool slightly. Puree the vegetables and some of the liquid in a blender or food processor. Pour the puree back into the remaining liquid. Remove the bay leaf and heat soup thoroughly before serving. Serves 4.

SPINACH AND GARLIC SOUP

1 tablespoon (15ml) extra virgin olive oil

1 head garlic, separated into cloves and peeled

2 onions, chopped

3 bay leaves

1 tablespoon (15ml) minced fresh thyme

2 allspice berries, crushed

3 cups chicken or beef stock

1 cup milk

1 cup shredded fresh spinach

In a large pot, warm oil over medium heat. Add garlic, onions, bay leaves, thyme, and allspice, and sauté until onion just begins to get translucent, about 10 minutes. Add stock, and bring to a boil. Reduce heat to simmer, and cook until garlic is tender, about 15 minutes. Discard bay leaves, and use a slotted spoon to transfer garlic and onions to a food processor or blender. Add a splash of stock and process until smooth. Add garlic mixture to stock in the pot, and warm over low heat while adding milk. Continue to heat gently and stir until the soup is hot. Add spinach, stir briefly, then serve. Serves 2.

Main Dishes

BROILED FISH WITH BASIL BUTTER

4 one-inch (2.5cm)-thick fish steaks weighing approximately 2 pounds (1kg) total (use halibut, redfish, salmon, sea bass, shark, swordfish, tuna, or whitefish)

½ cup (125ml) softened butter or margarine

1 tablespoon (15ml) minced fresh basil

1 tablespoon (15ml) minced fresh parsley

2 teaspoons (10ml) lemon juice

¼ teaspoon (1.25ml) salt

In a small bowl, combine butter, basil, parsley, lemon juice, and salt, and mix

Remove fish from broiler, and spoon remaining butter mixture over it to serve. Serves 4.

ROAST CHICKEN WITH THYME AND MUSTARD

4 boneless, skinless chicken breasts

½ cup (125ml) plain bread crumbs

3 tablespoons (45ml) Dijon mustard

2 tablespoons (30ml) butter, melted

2 tablespoons (30ml) minced shallots

¼ teaspoon (1.25ml) crushed red pepper

1 teaspoon (5ml) minced fresh thyme

3 tablespoons (45ml) water

Pinch of salt

Mix mustard, melted butter, shallots, red pepper, thyme, water, and salt in medium bowl, and put aside 2 tablespoons (30ml) of resulting sauce. Dip chicken in sauce, and roll in bread crumbs. Place in buttered baking dish, and bake uncovered for 30 minutes at 350°F (180°C). Spoon reserved sauce over chicken, and serve. Serves 4.

well. Place steaks on greased rack of an unheated broiler pan. Brush fish with the butter mixture, and broil 4 inches (10cm) from the heat for 5 minutes. Turn fish, and brush with more of the mixture. Broil for 3 to 7 more minutes, until fish flakes easily when tested with a fork.

To take parsley away from the cook
would make it almost impossible for him
to exercise his art.

Louis Augustin Bose d'Antic

HERBED POT ROAST WITH VEGETABLES

4-pound (1.8 kg) boneless beef chuck roast, trimmed of fat

2 cloves garlic, crushed

1½ teaspoons (7.5ml) minced fresh marjoram

1 teaspoon (5ml) chopped fresh basil

1 teaspoon (5ml) salt

¼ teaspoon (1.25ml) freshly ground black pepper

¼ cup (60ml) apple cider

¼ cup (60ml) water

1 cup chopped celery, cut into 1-inch [2.5cm]-long pieces

5 medium carrots, cut into 2-inch (5cm)-long pieces

4 medium turnips, quartered

1 medium onion, quartered

1 green bell pepper, cut into 1-inch (2.5cm)-long pieces

2 tablespoons (30ml) chopped fresh parsley

Grease a Dutch oven, and cook beef over medium heat until brown, about 10 minutes. Sprinkle with garlic, marjoram, basil, salt, and black pepper. Add cider and water. Heat to boiling, then reduce heat. Cover, and simmer 1½ hours. Add vegetables, parsley, and if necessary, ¼ cup (60ml) water. Cover again, and simmer for about 45 minutes, until vegetables and beef are tender. Serves 6 to 8.

Stretching out a bony hand,
the old man pleaded,
Pay me with Dill Seed rare,
so my cupboard will not be bare.

Regimen Sanitatis Salerni, 10th-century Italy

Vegetables, Side Dishes, and Appetizers

NEW POTATOES WITH ROSEMARY

2 pounds (1kg) small red potatoes (plum size)

2 tablespoons (30ml) extra virgin olive oil

2 tablespoons (30ml) fresh rosemary leaves

1 teaspoon (5ml) salt

Boil whole potatoes for 12 to 15 minutes, until tender. Drain, and cool slightly. Place warm potatoes in serving bowl, and toss with oil, rosemary, and salt. Serve warm. Serves 4.

HERBED GREEN BEANS

1 pound (.45kg) fresh green beans, tips removed

2 tablespoons (30ml) extra virgin olive oil

¼ cup (60ml) chopped fresh parsley

1½ teaspoons (7.5ml) chopped fresh basil leaves

1½ teaspoons (7.5ml) chopped fresh oregano leaves

⅛ teaspoon (.06ml) crushed red pepper

2 cloves garlic, minced

Salt

Boil beans in salted water for 5 minutes, uncovered. Cover, and cook 5 to 10 minutes longer, until crisply tender. Drain. Heat oil in large skillet. Cook and stir remaining ingredients until garlic is golden. Add beans, and cook for 1 to 2 minutes, stirring occasionally, until beans are hot and coated with mixture. Serves 4.

VEGETABLE SHISH KABOB

¼ cup (60ml) extra virgin olive oil

¼ cup (60ml) red wine

4 cloves garlic, minced

¼ cup (60ml) balsamic vinegar

1 tablespoon (15ml) minced fresh basil

1 tablespoon (15ml) minced fresh oregano

1 small eggplant, cubed

24 whole mushrooms

2 red bell peppers, cut into 12 chunks

2 red onions, cut into large chunks

4 cups hot cooked basmati rice

In a shallow pan, combine oil, wine, garlic, vinegar, basil, and oregano. Add vegetables, cover, and marinate in the refrigerator for 24 hours, basting several times. Place an assortment of vegetables on each skewer, and grill or broil until lightly browned all over, basting a few times with leftover marinade. Serve over hot rice. Serves 4.

FRENCH HERBED CHEESE

2 eight-ounce (225g) packages cream cheese, softened

¼ pound (120g) butter, softened

2 tablespoons (30ml) Worcestershire sauce

1 tablespoon (15ml) whipping cream

2 teaspoons (10ml) lemon juice

1 clove garlic, minced

2 teaspoons (10ml) minced fresh chives

2 teaspoons (10ml) minced fresh parsley

1 teaspoon (5ml) minced fresh dill weed

½ teaspoon (2.5ml) minced fresh basil

½ teaspoon (2.5ml) minced fresh thyme

½ teaspoon (2.5ml) minced fresh tarragon

½ teaspoon (2.5ml) celery seeds

3 dashes hot pepper sauce

Salt and pepper to taste

Mix cream cheese and butter in the bowl of a food processor, or place in a large bowl and mix well by hand. Add all other ingredients and process or stir by hand until mixture is well blended. Add more whipping cream, if needed, to smooth out mixture. Spoon mixture into a mold or mound on serving plate, and refrigerate overnight. Serve at room temperature with crackers. Makes about 3 cups (750ml).

This flower takes off diseases,
In sickness gently pleases;
Its old age cannot sever
The scent it loses never;
And dead we keep for ever
The perfumed air of Roses fair.

Anacreon

chapter two

Herbs for Health and Healing

BUT FIRST, AN IMPORTANT CAVEAT!

The Chinese have nearly two thousand herbal remedies that they have been using for centuries. Marco Polo wrote of the herbs he found on his journey to China. The ancient Greek physicians created illustrated written accounts of uses for herbs, including St.-John's-wort, which is enjoying a renewed popularity today. Herbs were the primary medicines for every society until the nineteenth and early twentieth centuries, when scientists discovered how to synthesize many of the active ingredients in herbs and combine them into pharmaceuticals.

These modern versions of the old cures eventually took the place of herbal remedies. However, many people are now returning to the "old ways" and using herbs to prevent and cure ailments. They believe that these natural remedies may be safer than their synthetic counterparts, which can have unpredictable and unpleasant side effects. Just remember that for anything that pertains to your body and physical well-being, it really is better to be safe than sorry. Research any herb that you're considering taking for medicinal purposes, talk to your doctor about it, and keep the following advice in mind.

✦ Experimenting with herbal remedies can be dangerous. Many herbs are toxic even in small doses; some are deadly. Tobacco and marijuana, for instance, are herbs. Manufacturers in the United States are not allowed to make medical claims for herbal remedies, and for good reason. They are not recognized by the U.S. Food and Drug Administration and, therefore, are not subject to any inspection, quality control, or testing.

✦ If you decide to use herbal remedies, be sure that you consult a physician who has experience in dispensing them, and that you obtain them from a reputable herbalist or homeopathic pharmacy selling high-quality products. Herbal remedies are not to be confused with homeopathic remedies, which are dilutions of highly toxic substances and should be taken only under the direction of a homeopathic physician. These substances, which are regulated by the FDA, can be extremely dangerous if used improperly.

✦ Combining several herbs or using herbs and prescription pharmaceuticals together may cause dangerous reactions. Tell your physician or herbalist about any medications or herbs you may be taking, and ask his or her advice before starting to use an herbal remedy.

✦ Many of the remedies in this book, such as eucalyptus, are for external use only and must not be ingested. Please read this book and all other information about herbal remedies very carefully before using herbs for medicinal purposes.

TRADITIONAL HERBAL REMEDIES

Many healing herbs are mentioned in literature, from ancient Greek texts to the Bible, as well as in Shakespeare's writings. Here is a list of herbs used in traditional remedies and their general applications.

Aloe vera (gel, external use only): **Soothes burns, sunburn, diaper rash**

Aloe vera (capsules): **Aids intestinal health, immune system**

Anise: **Eases lung congestion, coughs, flatulence**

Arnica (ointment, external use only): **Reduces inflammation and pain of sore muscles, bruises, and strains**

Basil (fresh): **Soothes insect stings when used as a poultice**

Basil (ingested): **Reduces nausea**

Color of cinnamon
Clove's sweet smell
I've come a long way
To see Gabrielle

Jorge Amado

Bay leaf: **Eases lung congestion, coughs**

Blackberry leaf (tea): **Alleviates diarrhea**

Burdock (tea): **Aids liver and kidneys in detoxification**

Burdock (skin wash): **Helps heal eczema; fights bacterial and fungal infections**

Calendula (cream, external use only): **Soothes dry skin, diaper rash**

Caraway: **Reduces flatulence, menstrual cramps**

Cardamom: **Eases heartburn; combats halitosis**

Catnip: **Aids relaxation**

Chamomile (tea): **Reduces tension, stress, indigestion**

Comfrey (cream, external use only): **Stops bleeding; soothes skin abrasions and rashes**

Coriander (oil, used externally): **Eases joint pain**

Cumin (tea): **Fights flu and colds; reduces muscle spasms**

Dandelion (tea): **Promotes liver health; acts as a diuretic and laxative**

Dill: Eases gas, headaches, insomnia; combats halitosis

Echinacea (tea or extract): Helps prevent colds and flu; stimulates the immune system

Elderberry (tea): Fights flu, colds, hay fever

Elderberry (salves and skin washes, external use only): Helps heal cuts, burns, eczema

Eucalyptus (vapors): Relieves chest and nasal congestion

Eucalyptus (oil, external use only): Eases joint pain

Evening primrose (oil, ingested): Reduces premenstrual symptoms; helps heal eczema

Fennel (tea): Reduces nausea and symptoms of food poisoning

Feverfew (tea, extract): Alleviates migraines and headaches

Garlic (capsules, oil, or fresh): Helps prevent colds, high blood pressure, high cholesterol

Gentian (extract): Increases the appetite and stimulates digestion; reduces fevers, induces menstruation

Ginger (tea, capsules): Reduces motion sickness, nausea, fever

Ginger (liniment, used externally): Soothes arthritis and sore muscles, stimulates blood circulation

Gingko (tea, capsules): Increases blood circulation for improved alertness and memory; may help asthma and vertigo

Ginseng (tea, capsules): Boosts energy

Goldenseal (extract): Lowers blood pressure; destroys many viral and bacterial infections; reduces inflammation of mucous-membrane areas

Horehound (tea, extract): Soothes coughs and bronchitis; reduces fever

Hyssop (tea): Relieves cold and flu symptoms

Lavender (aromatic oil, external use only): Reduces stress, jet lag; fights bacterial and fungal infections

Lemon balm (tea): Fights depression and bacterial infections

Lemon balm (cream, external use only): Soothes cold sores

Lemongrass (tea): Reduces nasal and sinus congestion, soothes indigestion

Licorice (tea, extract): Soothes stomach ailments, throat irritations, coughs, liver ailments; regulates menstruation

Milk thistle (tea or capsules): Helps with liver ailments

Nettle (tea): Reduces anemia; increases circulation; helps heal eczema

Oregano (ingested): Reduces vertigo, motion sickness

Papaya (tea): Aids digestion; reduces nausea

Parsley (fresh, ingested): Combats halitosis

Peppermint (tea, aromatic oil): Relieves sinus congestion; aids digestion

Raspberry leaf (tea): Soothes menstrual cramps

Rosemary (aromatic oil): Alleviates jet lag, headaches, muscle soreness

Rosemary (tea): Relieves nasal and sinus congestion; combats dandruff when used externally

Rose water (lotion, external use only): Soothes skin irritations; reduces tension

Saffron: Reduces coughing spasms; eases gas

Sage (tea): Relieves nasal congestion; soothes sore throat

Sage (oil, external use only): Repels insects

St.-John's-wort (extract, pills): Fights depression, insomnia, anxiety, menstrual cramps; reduces pain and inflammation

Sesame (oil, external use only): Alleviates dry skin

Spearmint (tea): Aids digestion; relieves nasal and sinus congestion

Tarragon (fresh, ingested): Stimulates appetite; eases insomnia

Thyme (oil): Fights bacteria when used as a mouthwash, skin lotion, or gargle

Valerian (tea, capsules): Eases insomnia, headaches

Yarrow (tea): Relieves nasal and sinus congestion; increases circulation; lowers blood pressure

O Great Spirit! do not go away.
I have come with a clean hart.
My soul is unstained.
It is purged of sin and wicked design.
Remain here, O Greatest of Spirits.

Chinese prayer to ginseng

I know a bank whereon the wild thyme blows,
Where ox-lips and the nodding violet grows.

William Shakespeare, *A Midsummer Night's Dream*

SOOTHING HERBAL TEAS

Literally hundreds of herbal teas are available at health-food stores and homeopathic pharmacies, so be good to yourself and bring home a variety. Savor one at a time until you discover your favorites. If you decide to make tea with your home-grown herbs, be sure to determine first whether the herb you've chosen is safe to ingest.

✦ Use 1 ounce (30g) of dried herbs or 2¹/₂ ounces (75g) of fresh herbs to 2 cups (500ml) of water. If you're using fresh herbs, chop them finely so that their flavor and medicinal properties will be released.

✦ Place the herbs in a teapot, and pour the boiling water over them. Cover tightly, and steep for at least 10 minutes. Strain into a teacup.

✦ You may use one serving and refrigerate the other for later use, but do not store herbal infusions in the fresh food section of the refrigerator for

more than 24 hours; make a fresh pot of tea each day.

✦ If you want to store your herbal teas for a longer period of time, make a more concentrated version of the above by using 3 tablespoons (45ml) of fresh herbs per cup (250ml) of water, and freeze the mixture in an ice cube tray. You can then drop the frozen cubes into a cup of hot water for instant herbal tea.

With uses too many to mention,
   Malaria's one target of gentian.
Connoisseurs are surer
   To sip Angostura,
Which helps many things more than tension!

James A. Duke

✦ Try flavoring your regular or herbal teas with honey, lemon juice and zest, orange juice and zest, cinnamon sticks, slices of fresh ginger, or whole cloves.

chapter three

Herb Gardening, Indoors and Out

IN THE KNOW ABOUT GROWING HERBS

If you're new to gardening, though you may be eager to have a mind-boggling herb garden just outside your kitchen door, you are better off starting small; plant just a few herbs that you know and love or can learn about easily, and grow only those that you use frequently. For the more experienced gardener, the sky's the limit! You may wish to plant one herb garden for cooking, one for drying herbs to use in crafts and flower arrangements, and perhaps even an old-style "physic" garden for herbal home remedies and beauty preparations.

Why should he die, whose garden groweth sage?
No other plant with death such stife can wage.
Sage soothes the nerves, and stills a trembling hand,
And sharpest fevers fly at his command.
The beaver, sage and lavender will bring,
With tansy, and the cress, first gifts of spring.

Regimen Sanitatis Salerni, 10th-century Italy

✦ Ideally, your "kitchen" herb garden should be in a spot near the kitchen door so you'll be able to pick the herbs on the spur of the moment as you're cooking. However, there's something to be said for placing herbs among the flower beds and other plantings. Then, when a recipe calls for a sprig of thyme, you can wander through the whole garden and enjoy the break your herb gathering task has afforded.

✦ Generally, herbs want a spot with plenty of sun (six to eight hours a day) and good drainage, whether they're planted indoors or out. Don't overwater—many herbs, especially those of Mediterranean origin, are adapted to a semiarid climate and don't like "wet feet." In addition, too much water will dilute the fragrance and flavor of the herbs, thus defeating the whole purpose of your garden.

✦ If you're in a growing zone with frequent summer rains, you may not need to water your herb garden at all, but keep a close watch. If the leaves look the slightest bit limp, you've waited too long—water immediately! In more arid zones, water 2 or 3 times a week. A drip irrigation system is an ideal solution for an herb garden that requires watering. Consider putting it on an automatic timer.

✦ Such herbs as rosemary and sage will tolerate more shade and a somewhat richer soil, and mint even likes a damp spot. Read the seed packets or seedling tags carefully to determine the sun and water requirements of each plant.

✦ Buy an inexpensive soil-testing kit from your local nursery, and check the pH of your garden spot. An herb garden grows best in neutral soil, so you may need to add lime if your soil is too acidic, or sulfur if it's too alkaline.

✦ Plant herbs with similar needs for sun and water near each other. This move will save you time in caring for them and will enable you to avoid the situation of having one herb make a neighboring one unhappy with too much or too little sun or water.

✦ Many herbs like a somewhat sandy soil, and your own compost is the best soil amendment to provide a good growing medium. If you compost when you plant, you probably won't need to feed your

herb garden any fertilizer, as these plants are quite hardy and have adapted to poor conditions.

✦ Use mulch, such as wood chips or colorful gravel, to keep weeds down.

✦ Keep the garden weeded and clear of debris to discourage pests.

✦ Remember, you're going to eat the leaves of most of these plants, so never use toxic sprays on them to control weeds, pests, or plant diseases.

✦ Many herbs are natural pest repellents. Such pests as aphids can usually be controlled by gently washing the leaves with water and mild soap. Try using benign methods, such as placing a saucer of beer to trap snails and slugs or deploying a pint of helpful, beautiful ladybugs to attack aphids and other pests. Consult your local nursery for other organic solutions for your specific plants and growing area.

✦ Many herbs, such as dill, coriander, basil, chervil, and parsley, can be grown from seed, but if your growing zone is in the cooler climes, seedlings from your local nursery will give you a head start.

✦ Keep seedlings in a cold frame for a week to acclimate them to the cool nights, and put them in the ground after the last frost. If a surprise late frost threatens, cover the seedlings with sheets of plastic overnight.

✦ Plants that don't germinate successfully from seed, such as tarragon, bay, and lavender, can be started by dividing the roots and planting small clumps. Ask a friendly herb gardener for some rootstock. Rootstock can sometimes be purchased from nurseries; if all else fails, you can try taking cuttings from another plant.

✦ Don't forget to put identifying labels on the plants so you'll know what you're harvesting. For a personal touch, design and paint your own wooden herb signs, perhaps including a sketch of the plant as it will look in its mature state.

✦ If a plant seems exhausted before the growing season is over, replace it!

✦ If you have a sunny spot where you can plant several square feet (1–2 square m) of herbs, try creating your own garden design. There are a number of excellent books on classic herb garden designs, such as knots, cartwheels, and other geometric patterns.

✦ Knot gardens are formally designed spaces, usually square in shape, in which the low-growing bordering hedges cross each other in intricate patterns that make the hedges appear "knotted." Various herbs are planted in the open spaces within the design, and the hedges help to contain their growth. In large gardens, several squares of these "knots" may be placed adjacent to one another for a grand design.

✦ Cartwheel garden designs are based on a circular pattern, usually with a centrally located point of interest, such as a classical statue or animal sculpture, a fountain, a birdbath, a Victorian gazing globe, a sundial, or an ornamental tree. A statue of St. Fiacre, the patron saint of herbs, would be an apt choice. Border hedges or paths radiate out like spokes from the center of the cartwheel, and the pie-shaped spaces in between are planted with herbs to provide a palette of colors and aromas.

✦ Bear in mind that a great amount of care and trimming is required to keep the patterns in a formal garden design neat. Unless you have daily help in the garden, you might prefer a less demanding design.

✦ Try your hand at "painting" with herbs, and plant a "meadow" design of different colors and textures. Though carefully planned, this garden has a wilder, cottage-garden look to it and does not require a lot of pruning and trimming.

✦ If space is minimal, consider a border garden of herbs planted along a fence or sidewalk.

✦ Even for the smallest space, always draw garden plans first. Consider colors, watering requirements, and height, and keep the taller plants—such as dill, lavender, and lemongrass—in the center of the

design or at the back of a border garden for easy harvesting.

✦ Once your plan is drawn, lay it out with stakes and string on the actual plot. Walk around and visualize the garden.

✦ If you cannot easily reach every part of the garden from the outside borders to weed, water, and harvest, then plan paths and/or stepping stones for access.

✦ If your garden doesn't look the way you visualized it once it's planted and growing, don't panic. Herbs are quite hardy and are easily transplanted. Just dig up the plant carefully, trying not to disturb or cut off roots, and move it to the spot of your choice.

✦ Plant some extra ground-cover herbs like creeping rosemary, mint, or thyme along the paths so they will give off their fragrance

when stepped on. The wealthiest ancient Romans sometimes covered an entire floor or even a city street with the leaves of aromatic herbs to mask unpleasant odors.

✦ You can even grow a whole fragrant lawn of some varieties of chamomile and thyme. These plants don't need mowing, and they contribute beautiful flowers, as well as delicious scents.

✦ Low-growing herbs also make attractive borders around the vegetable garden or flower bed, but be sure not to plant them near any flowers that will be sprayed with toxic chemicals.

✦ Have a lot of space? Be sure to include a bench or garden seat to provide a peaceful, fragrant place for reading a book or just daydreaming.

✦ Once you're hooked on herb gardening, try growing some of the more exotic varieties of your old favorites: purple or cinnamon basil, golden oregano, tricolor sage, chocolate mint, or some of the many different varieties of mint, basil, thyme, rosemary, and chamomile.

✦ If you're ambitious, try creating a topiary with rosemary. The trailing, "creeping" variety lends itself to wrapping around topiary forms; it can also be espaliered or trellised. Other candidates for miniature topiary projects are bay, lemon verbena, thyme, and lavender. This kind of training may take years of pruning and attention, so be patient!

TIPS ON SOME FAVORITES

Aloe vera: Sometimes called "the first aid plant," aloe vera is not only one of the most useful herbal remedy plants, but also one of the easiest to grow. A tropical succulent that likes rich soil, partial shade, and good drainage, aloe should only be watered when dry. It is virtually pest-free. Feed it every other month if it's in a pot, transplanting it into larger containers as it grows. If you're in a frost zone, cover it or bring pots inside in winter, as frost will kill aloe. This plant will continue to thrive in a sunny window or under a fluorescent "grow light." To harvest, cut one of the large "leaves" at the bottom of the plant. Slice the leaf lengthwise to expose the gelatinous flesh, and apply the flesh or gel directly to cuts, scrapes, rashes, and minor burns. (If the burn is serious enough to cause an open wound, see a doctor immediately.) This is an excellent sunburn remedy. It can also be used as a facial mask or hair conditioner.

Basil: This indispensable herb loves a sunny spot, but watch for aphids. Keep the buds pinched back to create a fuller, bushier plant with more leaves. Doing so will also prevent it from "bolting" or shooting up and going to seed in the heat.

Chive: Pretty pink flowers and dark green leaves make this plant a good choice for a border. It grows easily from seeds and by division of its bulb clusters. This plant is an excellent choice for container gardening.

Coriander: Also known as cilantro and Chinese parsley, fresh coriander leaves are a favorite seasoning in many Asian and Latin American cuisines. The seeds are also used as a seasoning, so let some of your plants go to seed and collect them after the stalks have grown brittle. Coriander grows well from seed and may reach a height of three feet (1m), so put it behind the smaller plants in your garden.

Dill: This annual is easily grown from seed, and will spill enough seed so that you have "volunteer" plants the following

> Rue, myrrh, and cummin for the sphinx
> Her muddy eye to clear.
>
> Ralph Waldo Emerson

spring. Dill can grow up to five feet (1.5m) tall, so keep it behind the shorter plants in the garden.

Garlic: Buy garlic "sets" from your nursery in the spring, and plant the separated, unpeeled cloves 1 to 2 inches (2.5 to 5cm) deep and 6 inches (15cm) apart. Harvest when the leaves begin to droop. Braid the stems together and hang in your kitchen.

Lavender: No true herb garden is complete without this beautiful, fragrant favorite. It should be propagated from stem cuttings or clumps of roots, as it does not germinate well from seeds.

Mint: There are hundreds of varieties of mint, but the most popular are spearmint and peppermint. Mint is a hardy perennial and is very invasive in a garden, so it should always be grown in a contained space.

Oregano: There are many varieties of oregano, which is closely related to marjoram. Try sweet marjoram or the hybrid Italian oregano, both of which grow well in containers.

And rosemarine,
  I lett it run all over my garden walls,
Not onlie because my bees love it,
  But because 'tis the herb
Sacred to remembrance
  And, therefore, to friendship.
                          Sir Thomas More

Parsley: Parsley is a biennial (living two years), but in the second season the growth flowers and goes to seed, so it's best to treat it as an annual and replant each year. It makes beautiful borders and grows well in a pot.

Rosemary: Since rosemary does not germinate well, try propagating it from tip cuttings. If you live in an area with cold winters, plant rosemary in a pot that can be taken inside during the winter months.

Sage: This plant has woody stems. It is best propagated from stem cuttings and clumps of root division. Although considered a perennial, it needs to be replanted every two or three years.

Tarragon: Don't bother attempting to grow tarragon from seed; it should only be propagated from cuttings. And be sure you have French tarragon, not the weed-like and tasteless Russian variety.

Thyme: There are so many varieties of thyme, you could devote an entire herb garden to them—and some people do! The old standby for seasoning is English thyme, but try planting several of the low-growing varieties for a lawn "carpet" of many colors. Propagate this plant by root division.

CONTAINING YOUR PASSION FOR HERB GARDENING

Containers overflowing with herbs fit perfectly on a back porch, patio, balcony, or even a sunny windowsill. Herbs in hanging baskets under a skylight will thank you with year-round fragrance and flavor. You can even grow herbs indoors using fluorescent grow lights, though remember that indoor herbs will not have quite the pungency of herbs grown in natural light.

✦ If you're growing herbs in pots, use soil that has a slightly alkaline pH reading and good drainage, and be sure to water before the soil dries out. Be sure you don't overwater, since this action kills more container plants than any disease or pest.

✦ Large containers made of porous materials are best, as most herbs have complex root systems and all need good drainage.

✦ If you're really cramped for space, try filling the many pockets of a strawberry

only organic fertilizers, such as fish emulsion, as the plants will absorb chemicals from whatever you feed them or use to amend the soil.

✦ Herbs that are well suited for container gardening include:

>   **anise, basil,* bay, caraway,**
>   **chives, cilantro, cumin,**
>   **dill (fern leaf variety),**
>   **fennel,* French tarragon,***
>   **lavender, lemongrass, mint,**
>   **oregano, parsley, *creeping**
>   **rosemary,* sage, sorrel,**
>   **thyme, and winter savory.**

*needs grow lights if grown indoors

planter with a variety of your favorite herbs for a whole garden in one pot.

✦ Planting parsley or creeping rosemary in a hanging basket can save space.

✦ Herbs growing in pots will be happy with a monthly feeding. Consider using

And (she) took especial pride to sleek
  Her lightsome locks of hair;
With rosemary when she wreathed them . . .

Ovid

Lavender's blue, dilly dilly, lavender's green
When I am king, dilly dilly, you shall be queen.

English rhyme

HARVEST TIME

✦ To harvest herbs, pick them just as they are forming buds and before they flower; this is when they are at their flavor peak. Pick them in the morning, just after the dew has dried and before the heat of the day prompts them to release their essential oils and flavors. Carefully wash and dry the herbs, and pick off any dead or discolored leaves.

✦ Most herbs should be harvested by pinching off just the amount of leaves or sprigs that you will use immediately, since herbs quickly lose their freshness and flavor after they have been picked.

✦ Do not pull the plants up by the roots. Herbs will continue to grow and give you weeks of enjoyment if you keep them pinched back. If you're harvesting a large quantity to dry, don't take all the leaves from one plant, but pick a few sprigs from several different plants to keep them all growing. You can cut a plant back by as much as one half if you must. Many herbs will grow fuller with constant pruning.

✦ To harvest seeds, such as dill or coriander, tie a small paper or plastic bag over the head of the plant when the seeds look ready to fall, then gently bend the plant toward the ground and shake the head to dislodge the seeds into the bag.

✦ To harvest roots and bulbs, wait until the plant's leaves have died at the end of the season.

TIPS ON PRESERVING AND STORING HERBS

Storing Fresh Herbs

✦ Fresh bouquets of such herbs as parsley, sage, basil, oregano, rosemary, and thyme can be stored in glasses of water in the refrigerator, much like bouquets of flowers. Put a rubber band around the bottom of the stems to hold each bouquet upright, and cover loosely with a clear plastic bag. This treatment will keep the herbs fresh as water condenses inside the bag. Snip the stem ends and change the water daily.

✦ Try not to harvest more of any fresh herb than you will use in 24 hours. Freshly picked herbs are best!

> For you there's rosemary and rue;
> these keep seeming and savor all the winter long.
>
> William Shakespeare, *The Winter's Tale*

Freezing Leafy Herbs

✦ Remove the stems, wash the leaves in cold water, and pat dry with paper towels or spin them in a salad spinner. Chop leaves in a food processor, slowly adding water or, if you prefer, extra virgin olive oil to achieve a pasty consistency. Make a large enough batch to freeze in an ice cube tray, and once frozen, store the cubes in freezer bags or plastic containers. The cubes can be dropped into soups and sauces or defrosted in the microwave and used to pep up salad dressings or sauces. Don't be deterred by the black color of frozen basil; this herb will retain its flavor.

✦ Leafy herbs may also be frozen without water or oil. Wash and dry the leaves, spread in a single layer on a cookie sheet, and freeze until hard, about one hour. Put the amount of frozen leaves you think you'll use at one time into individual sandwich-size plastic bags. Squeeze the air out of the bags, and pack several together in a larger freezer bag for protection from freezer burn.

Drying Herbs

✦ Though any fresh herb can be a delightful addition to your recipes, some herbs are actually more potent when dried.

✦ To dry long-stemmed herbs, such as marjoram, mint, parsley, rosemary, sage, and savory, tie the stems into a small bundle and hang in a cool, dry, dark place. The beams in the garage or basement would work well, or perhaps in an attic or a gardening shed, or even inside a closet or pantry. Tie the bottom of the stems tightly, as they'll shrink during drying and may fall out of the bunch.

✦ Air circulation is an important factor in successful herb drying. The smaller the bundle, the quicker the herbs will dry, and the more their flavor will be preserved.

✦ Herbs can even be dried outdoors if they are not subjected to direct sunlight or water. To keep them dust-free, tie each bunch inside a small paper bag,

Lavender, sweet blooming lavender,
Six bunches a penny to-day.
Lavender, sweet blooming lavender,
Ladies buy it while you may.

Old London street cry

✦ Your microwave oven can also be used to dry herbs, but be sure to remove all excess moisture after rinsing them—otherwise they'll cook instead of dry. Place a few pieces between two paper towels and run the oven on high for two to three minutes. Check the herbs to see if they're completely dry. If not, repeat for thirty-second intervals until they're ready to store.

make a few holes in the bag, and cut off the bottom of the bag to provide air circulation.

✦ To dry shorter stems that can't easily be tied in bundles or to dry seeds and large-leafed herbs, use screens, cheese-cloth, or large trays such as cookie sheets or pizza pans. Wash and dry the herbs, and spread a single layer of leaves or seeds on the trays, leaving enough space between the herbs for good air circulation. Gently rearrange and turn them every few days, and in about a week, they should be crisp and dry.

✦ As a last resort, you can oven-dry herbs in a stove oven or even a toaster oven at the very lowest setting, but the herbs will not retain as much of their flavor as naturally dried ones.

✦ When the herbs are completely crisp and dry, place them in screw-top jars and close tightly. If you see any evidence of mold or insects, discard the herbs.

✦ Crush the dried herbs just at the point you want to use them, and not before, to release their flavor.

chapter four

Herbal Treasures

CREATE MAGNIFICENT HERBAL WREATHS, SWAGS, AND GARLANDS

Create unique gifts from the bounty of your herb garden, or indulge your own love of herbs. Certain herbs have specific associations. Rosemary, for instance, has special significance at Christmas. It is said that the Virgin Mary spread her blue cloak on a rosemary bush when the Holy Family stopped to rest on their flight from Bethlehem and that since then, rosemary has bloomed with a blue flower in her honor.

✦ If you're looking forward to using the bounty of your herb garden to create craft items, be sure to plant enough bay. Bay leaves are indispensable in making wreaths and other dried arrangements. These sturdy herbs not only retain a green color, but they withstand handling and arranging without crumbling.

✦ If you don't have a eucalyptus tree, make friends with someone who does. These wonderful, pungent leaves are a staple in wreaths and garlands. There are many varieties of eucalyptus, but look for the leaves shaped like knife blades and the beautiful "spiral" or "silver-dollar" varieties in particular. They look wonderful combined with your favorite dried flowers.

✦ Additional favorites for crafts are lavender, which retains its wonderful fragrance even when dried, and such other aromatics as beautiful dusty-green sage and rosemary, with its pine-needlelike leaves.

✦ In addition to collecting dried herbs and flowers from your own garden, plan a picnic and harvest day with friends in the

Here of Sunday morning
My love and I would lie,
and I would turn and answer
Among the springing thyme.

A.E. Houseman, "The Shropshire Lad"

nearest meadow or woods. You'll find a treasure trove of beautiful grasses, bits of bark, berries, pinecones, seed pods, thistles, dried mosses and lichens, wildflowers, evergreen fronds, vines, and graceful branches. Many of these materials are available at craft shops, but purchasing them is not nearly as much fun as gathering them on your own treasure hunt. Remember to ask all the appropriate permissions and harvest responsibly. Never dig up native plants or break off branches of living trees. There are plenty of items that can be gathered without causing harm to any living things.

✦ Cover hollow wreath frames of wire, twigs, or dried vines with sphagnum or sheet moss that has been soaked to reconstitute it. (Wear gloves when handling the moss, as it can cause skin irritations.) Once the moss is formed around the wreath, cover it with plastic or florist's tape to keep it damp and in place.

✦ Straw wreath forms are easy to work with and well suited for dry arrangements. Bind your chosen items to the form with nylon fishing line, or use florist's pins to poke them into the straw.

✦ In some cases, you may want to create a wreath or garland of fresh materials and then dry the completed item, rather than constructing the adornment with the more delicate dried materials from the start.

✦ Don't overlook heart-shaped forms and other significant shapes for special occasions. Wreaths don't have to be perfectly round.

✦ Heavier items, such as pinecones, miniature gourds, fruits, or large flower heads, need to be wired to the wreath form with florist's wire. Smaller items may be attached to a small wooden pick with wire twist-ties and then thrust into the form or attached with glue. Insert bunches of herbs and flowers with their bases all pointing in the same direction as you work your way around the wreath. Overlap them as you go to cover the base completely, and finish by gluing extra small bits into any open spots.

✦ Styrofoam wreath forms can be covered with moss to keep living herbs fresh. For dried arrangements, such forms can be spray-painted green or covered with green felt or some other type of sturdy fabric.

✦ Do not use a hot glue gun directly on Styrofoam; the heat may melt it. This caveat also applies to straw, which is flammable. Instead, apply the hot glue to the items you want to attach, then press them onto the wreath form.

✦ Start clipping! Many decorating books, magazines, and catalogs show lovely scenes of dried floral and herbal wreaths

over fireplaces, on chandeliers, and around candles. However, you should be aware that these items are highly flammable and should be placed well away from any open flame.

✦ Create a living wreath by planting your favorite herb seedlings around a wire wreath form covered with soaked sphagnum moss. Root the seedlings in the moss, and attach them with transparent fishing line; then pack another layer of moss over the roots. The moss needs to be sprayed daily to keep the herbs growing. This "fairy ring" is a lovely and useful addition to a kitchen garden.

✦ For winter holidays, add sprigs of your favorite fresh or dried aromatic herbs to pine wreaths and garlands to add texture and color and mingle the scents.

✦ Create a classic herb wreath with bay, chili peppers, mint, oregano, rosemary, sage, and thyme. Hang this one in the kitchen so that you can enjoy the aroma, and if you like, pick off pieces to use when you're cooking. (If you're going to use it that way, wire the pieces on rather than using glue.)

✦ For a fabulous red and green holiday wreath, combine dried sage and eucalyptus leaves, rosemary and tarragon sprigs, holly or bittersweet berries, and dried red chilies. Finish it off with a gold or red bow.

✦ Garlands and swags can be created using these same techniques. As a base, you can choose simple, natural-looking twines or rope, transparent high-test fishing line, wire, or something more decorative, such as braided raffia or sea grass. Be sure to choose a line that is strong enough to carry the weight of the materials on your garland.

✦ The longer the garland, the more stress the line will have to withstand, so choose your base with that in mind. A long garland will also need wire loops attached at intervals to help support its weight, and those should be incorporated into the foundation line before you begin to attach items.

✦ If you have especially heavy items and want the garland to last several seasons, invest in a colorful mountain climber's line of woven synthetic materials. If you can't find a climbing rope in a color that suits your plans, you can always wrap it with tape or fabric or cover it with sprigs of rosemary, bay, etc. You can then thread more delicate materials on high-test transparent fishing line and wind them around your strong foundation line.

✦ Use garlands on windows, across door frames, on the mantel, along stair railings, along the edges of shelves and cabinets, over mirrors and pictures, as table runners, or even on outside doors and windows to decorate your home's façade.

✦ If swags are to be draped over a door, window, or mantel, finish off the center with a beautiful ribbon bow or with a larger display of decorative items to provide a focal point at the center.

Above the lowley plants I towers
    The fennel, with its yellow flowers,
And in an earlier age than ours,
    Was gifted with the wondrous powers,
Lost vision to restore.

                    Henry Wadsworth Longfellow

PAMPERING WITH HERBS

Some believe that Cleopatra owed her beauty to the use of aloe. Throughout the ages, women—and a fair share of men as well—have used herbs as part of their daily personal care routine, stimulating their complexions with rosemary or relaxing with a soothing catnip bath. Whether you take pleasure in making a facial mask for yourself or a special gift for a friend, herbs offer a surprising variety of possibilities.

Herbal Bath Oils

First soften the water with a splash of cider vinegar, then try some of these essential oils from your local herb shop for special baths.

Bergamot: **Invigorates**

Calendula: **Slightly astringent; good for dry or itchy skin**

Catnip: **Relaxes**

Chamomile: **Slightly astringent; soothes skin; relaxes**

Eucalyptus: **Relieves congestion**

Fennel: **Slightly astringent; cleanses and invigorates**

Lavender: **Relaxes; good for oily skin and protecting female "yin" energy**

Lemon balm: **Soothes**

Lemon verbena: **Invigorates**

Lovage: **Deodorizes**

Marjoram: **Soothes**

Parsley: **Helpful for oily skin**

Peppermint: **Invigorates; promotes healing**

Rosemary: **Invigorates**

Rose water: **Creates a romantic ambience**

Sage: **Purifies; stimulates; slightly astringent**

Thyme: **Deodorizes; acts as an antiseptic**

Valerian: **Soothes**

Yarrow: **Cleanses; slightly astringent; good for oily skin**

Fresh Herb Baths

When you grow favorite aromatic herbs in pretty pots set on the bathroom windowsill, they are there for the picking when you're ready for a special bath. Tear or crush the leaves, and put them in a net bag. Then toss the bag into the tub while you fill the tub with water. For a more intense bath mixture, make an infusion with the herbs: chop ½ cup (125ml) fresh herbs, place them in a large jar or measuring cup, pour 1 quart (1l) of boiling water over them, and steep for 20 minutes. Strain the liquid into your bath as you fill the tub with water.

Bath Sachets

Combine dried lavender, rose petals, sage, and rosemary in a muslin or cheesecloth bag. Tie the bag under the faucet and let the water run through it, or float it in the water to scent your bath. Experiment with your own mixtures, and keep track of the ingredients by writing them on a little tag attached to each bag. Then, when you find a favorite "recipe," you can reproduce it. Keep a beautiful basket or bowl full of bath sachets handy by the tub.

Hair Care

Try aloe vera gel as a conditioner after shampooing. Leave on for 5 minutes and rinse thoroughly. Herbal vinegar makes a great hair rinse after shampooing

Your breath is sweeter than balm, sugar or licorice . . .
And yourself as sweet as the gillyflower
Or lavender seeds strewn in a coffer to smell.

Anonymous

and also helps to control dandruff. Add ½ cup (125ml) of white cider vinegar to 2 cups (500ml) of your chosen herbal infusion. Try chamomile and calendula to highlight blond hair, parsley and rosemary for dark hair, or sage as a purifier.

Facial Care

Apply fresh aloe gel to the face, avoiding the area around the eyes. Let the mask dry for 30 minutes, and rinse with cool water. Pat dry. An overnight application of aloe gel can be helpful in curing minor skin eruptions and rashes. To create your own skin toner, dilute white vinegar with 5 parts water, bring to a boil, and pour over crushed calendula, mint, or lavender. Let the herbs steep overnight. Then strain and pour into a sterilized bottle, and keep refrigerated. As with any astringent, avoid the eye area.

Herbal Mouthwash

Crush 3 tablespoons (45g) of fresh leaves of mint and/or rosemary in a mug, pour in 1 cup (250ml) of boiling water, and let cool. Gargle—but don't swallow—this very strong "tea" to refresh your breath.

Herbal Colognes

Try your hand at perfumery by adding crushed herbs and aromatic flowers to unscented rubbing alcohol. Pour 2 cups (500ml) of alcohol over approximately 1 cup (120g) of your chosen blend, and let the mixture sit in a tightly covered jar for several weeks at room temperature. Strain out the herbal material, and pour the cologne into a sterilized bottle. This is a perfect way to use those old perfume bottles you've been collecting.

Herbal Body Powder

- **1 cup (120g) powdered arrowroot**
- **1 cup (120g) cornstarch**
- **¼ cup (30g) baking soda**
- **2 tablespoons (30ml) of your favorite aromatic dried herbs, such as lavender or lemon balm, powdered or crushed**

Sift the ingredients together, and store in an airtight container.

QUICK CRAFT AND GIFT IDEAS

✦ When you create your own potpourri, you can experiment with many combinations of herbs, spices, and flowers. The two important considerations with potpourri are aroma and appearance. Since

Here's flowers for you
Hot lavender, mints, savory, marjoram;
The marigold that goes to bed with the sun
And with him, rises weeping.
William Shakespeare, *The Winter's Tale*

Saffron, 'tis said, brings comfort to mankind,
By giving rise to cheerfulness of mind.
Restores weak limbs, the liver also mends,
And normal vigor through its substance sends.

Ancient Italian verse

let the potpourri sit in the closed bag for at least 24 hours, but preferably several weeks, which will increase the intensity of the aroma. (Shake the mixture every few days.) Pour into a decorative bowl or basket for display. Try these aromatic herbs in creating your own potpourri recipes: anise, hyssop, basil, bay, cardamom, chamomile,

potpourri is usually displayed in open bowls and baskets, you'll want to add such natural ingredients as interesting seed pods, shells, or pinecones just for their visual appeal, even if they don't have special scents to impart to the mixture. Most potpourri recipes require the addition of a few drops of essential oils to bring out the fragrance. Combine the ingredients of your choice in a large bowl, add a fixative such as orrisroot or gum benzoin, and sprinkle the oils over the mixture. Pour the mixture into a plastic bag, toss gently, and lavender, lemon balm, lemongrass, lemon verbena, marjoram, mint, rosemary, sage, and thyme.

✦ To create herbal sachets, tie beautiful ribbons on cheesecloth or muslin bags filled with lavender, rose petals, chamomile, and calendula—or make your own favorite combinations to freshen dresser drawers and linen closets.

✦ Make decorative "sweet bags" of your favorite herbs to slip under your pillow or mattress. Or tie them to chairs and slip them between sofa cushions to freshen your living room.

✦ Kitchen hot pads that protect your table can be made by pulverizing favorite aromatic kitchen herbs and spices and filling pads sewn out of heavy fabric. The heat from a hot dish will release the kitchen sachet's aroma.

✦ Add cedar chips to a lavender, mint, and rosemary sachet to moth-proof dresser drawers or closets.

✦ Classic pomanders bring a spicy, warm scent to any room in winter. Use a toothpick or thin skewer to make a small hole next to the stem of an orange, and insert a clove until just the larger, star-shaped end is visible. Make the next hole just far enough from the first so that the star ends don't overlap, and continue until the whole orange is covered with cloves—no peel should be showing. The cloves will preserve the orange as it dries, and the pomander will last for months.

✦ To create a pomander-style holiday ornament for your home or for a gift, cover a Styrofoam ball with white glue, and roll the ball in finely crushed potpourri. Allow the glue to dry, then use a glue gun to affix other larger decorative items individually, such as bay leaves, cloves, small pieces of cinnamon stick, and flower petals. Decorate the covered ornaments with ribbons.

✦ For stove-top aromatics, try simmering this combination of dried herbs in an uncovered pan of water to send a beautiful aroma through your home: lemon verbena, sassafras twigs, cedar pieces, pine needles, cloves, allspice berries, and orange and lemon peels. For the winter holidays, use a mixture of rosemary, bay leaves, cinnamon sticks, cloves, and orange peel.

✦ You can make a cup of catnip tea for yourself, but don't forget your feline friends. Sew some dried leaves into a little cotton bag, and let your cat flip over it.

DECORATING WITH AN HERBAL THEME

There's something herbal for every room of your home. Whether the motive is aromatic or decorative, you'll get attractive, colorful, and satisfying results— and you won't have to take out a loan in the process!

✦ Use small plantings of herbs alongside "village blocks," miniature lighthouses, and other diminutive collections as part of the display. Do the same thing for a Nativity scene at Christmas.

✦ A hanging basket of aromatic herbs makes your front door welcoming at any time of year.

✦ Use your favorite cachepot, bread basket, silver bowl, or antique wooden boxes and bowls to hold nursery pots of herbs on windowsills.

✦ You can "create" an elegant and handsome instant tabletop topiary of your favorite herb. Choose a sturdy, straight

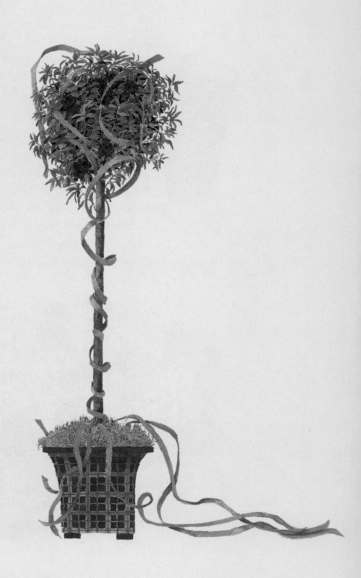

tree branch about 1½ inches (4cm) in diameter and 2 feet (60cm) long. A piece of beautiful white birch or smooth-skinned eucalyptus would be ideal, or you could even resort to a dowel or a piece of a broom handle and cover it in bay leaves. Cover a Styrofoam cone or ball 6 to 8 inches (15 to 20cm) in diameter with a thin layer of glue, and attach herbs and flowers of your choice. Leave a small uncovered space to glue the cone or ball to the branch tip. Anchor the branch in

Now the summer's in prime
 Wi' the flowers richly blooming.
And the wild mountain thyme
 A' the moorlands perfuming.
Robert Tannahill, "The Braes O' Balquhither"

> Poor Queen,
>   Here did she fall a tear; here in this place
> I'll set a bank of rue, sour herb of grace.
>   Rue, even for Ruth, shall shortly here be seen,
> In the remembrance of a weeping queen.
>
>   William Shakespeare, *Richard II*

florist's foam or packed sand in a decorative pot, and voilà—instant topiary!

✦ Add to the herbal theme in the kitchen or dining room with antique botanical prints of your favorites.

✦ Press your own herbs between sheets of blotting paper in a flower press. Use white glue to arrange them on heavy stock paper, then frame for a beautiful memento of your own garden.

✦ Collect Irish linen dish towels with herbal patterns to display in frames.

✦ Here's a perfect housewarming present or gift for a good cook: plant a variety of cooking herbs in a large, decorative pot. Attach a colorful pair of scissors to the pot with a ribbon for handy herb clipping.

✦ If you're so inclined, create herb stencils for walls and floor borders. Many home decorating stores carry tiles with herb designs, or you can paint your own and fire them at the local pottery kiln.

✦ Hang bundles of dried herbs as decorative elements in your kitchen.

✦ Buy a big, beautiful chart of herbs and their uses at your local homeopathic pharmacy or health-food store, and frame it.

✦ For a mini herb garden, fill your prettiest shallow basket with little individual pots of growing herbs. Trim with a beautiful ribbon, and place in the kitchen, dining room, or bath.

✦ Add flowering fresh herbs or dried sprigs to flower arrangements, or put together a whole basket of herbs for an aromatic centerpiece.

✦ Tuck sprigs of fresh rosemary, thyme, or another favorite herb into the napkin rings at a dinner party.